ELEPHANT

By Jenna Grodzicki

Consultant: Darin Collins, DVM
Director, Animal Health Programs, Woodland Park Zoo

BEARPORT
PUBLISHING

Minneapolis, Minnesota

Credits

Cover and title page, © Angelo Cavalli/Getty; 3, © Johan Swanepoel/Shutterstock; 4–5, © meanderingemu/Alamy; 6, © sevenke/Shutterstock; 7, © rhardholt/iStock; 8, © Marco__Piunti/iStock; 9, © iStock/Naephoto; 10–11, © Manoj Shah/Getty; 12, © zhu difeng/Shutterstock; 13, © Keren Su/China Span/Alamy; 14, © STUDIO 11/Shutterstock; 15, © RafSei/iStock; 17, © StuPorts/iStock; 18, © YolandaVanNiekerk/iStock; 19, © Adria Photography/Getty; 20–21, © Aelice/Shutterstock; 23, © WLDavies/iStock

President: Jen Jenson
Director of Product Development: Spencer Brinker
Senior Editor: Allison Juda
Associate Editor: Charly Haley
Designer: Colin O'Dea

Library of Congress Cataloging-in-Publication Data

Names: Grodzicki, Jenna, 1979- author.
Title: Elephant / by Jenna Grodzicki.
Description: Minneapolis, Minnesota : Bearport Publishing Company, [2022] | Series: Library of awesome animals | Includes bibliographical references and index.
Identifiers: LCCN 2020057396 (print) | LCCN 2020057397 (ebook) | ISBN 9781636911441 (library binding) | ISBN 9781636911526 (paperback) | ISBN 9781636911601 (ebook)
Subjects: LCSH: Elephants--Juvenile literature.
Classification: LCC QL737.P98 G76 2022 (print) | LCC QL737.P98 (ebook) | DDC 599.67--dc23
LC record available at https://lccn.loc.gov/2020057396
LC ebook record available at https://lccn.loc.gov/2020057397

For more information, write to Bearport Publishing, 5357 Penn Avenue South, Minneapolis, MN 55419.
Printed in the United States of America.

Contents

AWESOME
Elephants!

SPLASH! An elephant sprays water from its long trunk. Splashing and spraying on a hot summer day, elephants are awesome!

AN ELEPHANT'S TRUNK HAS ABOUT 40,000 MUSCLES. A HUMAN BODY HAS FEWER THAN 700!

Elephants are the largest land animals on Earth. In fact, an adult elephant can weigh as much as a school bus!

These huge **mammals** are found most often in the **grasslands** and forests of Africa and Asia. African elephants have bigger bodies than their Asian cousins. You can spot African elephants by their large ears shaped like the **continent** of Africa. Asian elephants have smaller ears that are more rounded.

An Asian elephant

ELEPHANTS FLAP THEIR LARGE EARS TO KEEP THEMSELVES COOL. THE EARS WORK A BIT LIKE BIG FANS.

An African elephant

The Nose Knows

Along with their large ears and big bodies, elephants are known for their trunks! Trunks are a long upper lip and nose all in one. Elephants use their trunks to suck up water and then spray it in their mouths. **SLURP!** But trunks can also act a lot like hands. Elephants can pick up food and other objects with their trunks. Awesome!

TWO ELEPHANTS MAY GREET EACH OTHER BY LINKING THEIR TRUNKS TOGETHER.

9

Follow the Leader

Elephants use their trunks to trumpet warnings. This comes in handy because elephants have a lot to tell one another. **Female** elephants often travel as a family.

The family group is called a **herd**. The leader of the herd is the **matriarch**. She is the oldest and largest female in the group.

AN ELEPHANT HERD TRAVELS IN A SINGLE-FILE LINE WITH THE MATRIARCH IN FRONT.

An Elephant Never Forgets

The matriarch has an important job to do. She decides where the herd should go to find food and water. So, it's good for her that she has the memory of . . . well, an elephant. A matriarch can remember the places where she has found food and water in the past. She leads the herd to the best spots to dine.

AN ELEPHANT'S MEMORY GOES BEYOND JUST FOOD. ELEPHANTS CAN RECOGNIZE OTHER ELEPHANTS—EVEN YEARS AFTER THE LAST TIME THEY WERE TOGETHER.

Dinner Time

Elephants are eating machines. They eat for an average of 16 hours every day. Grasses, leaves, fruits, and tree bark are all on the menu. *YUM!*

All that food can only mean one thing. Lots of poop! Elephants poop 12 to 15 times a day.

ELEPHANT POOP IS FULL OF SEEDS FROM THE PLANTS THEY EAT. THESE SEEDS CAN GROW INTO NEW PLANTS WHEREVER ELEPHANTS DO THEIR BUSINESS.

Danger!

A matriarch's memory can also protect the herd from danger. She can recognize things that may cause harm and then help the herd stay safe. While adult elephants have no natural **predators**, that doesn't mean they don't face **threats**. Sadly, the biggest harm to elephants comes from humans. For years, people have hunted elephants for their **tusks**.

ELEPHANTS ARE ALSO IN DANGER OF LOSING THEIR WILD LANDS AS HUMANS CLEAR NATURE TO MAKE WAY FOR NEW FARMS, ROADS, AND BUILDINGS.

A tusk

Oh, Baby

ROAR! Once a year, **male** elephants sound off as they join female herds to **mate**. But it will be almost two years before babies are born. Young calves have a lot to learn in their first few months. They practice using their trunks to pick up leaves and grasses. They learn how to spray themselves with water to keep clean.

CALVES LEARN TO EAT BY PUTTING THEIR TRUNKS INSIDE THEIR MOTHERS' MOUTHS TO TAKE FOOD.

Growing Up

A female calf will grow up and stay with the herd for her entire life. Male elephants remain with the herd until they are about 12 to 14 years old. Then, they go to live on their own or in small groups with other males. It may be another few years before they meet up with a herd again when it is time to mate.

ELEPHANTS LIVE LONGER THAN ANY OTHER LAND MAMMALS EXCEPT HUMANS. THEY CAN LIVE FOR UP TO 80 YEARS!

ELEPHANTS ARE AWESOME!
LET'S LEARN EVEN MORE ABOUT THEM.

Kind of animal: Elephants are mammals. Most mammals have fur, give birth to live young, and drink milk from their mothers as babies.

More elephants: There are different kinds of African elephants. Some live in savannas and others live in forests.

Size: Elephants are about 10 feet (3 m) tall. This is about the same size as a one-story house.

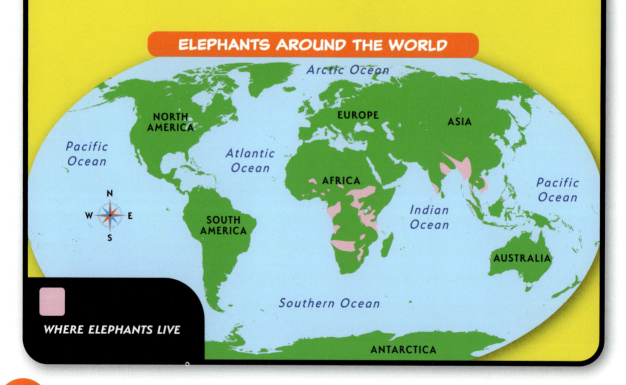

ELEPHANTS AROUND THE WORLD

Arctic Ocean

NORTH AMERICA

EUROPE

ASIA

Pacific Ocean

Atlantic Ocean

AFRICA

Indian Ocean

Pacific Ocean

SOUTH AMERICA

AUSTRALIA

Southern Ocean

WHERE ELEPHANTS LIVE

ANTARCTICA

continent one of the world's seven large land masses

female an elephant that can give birth to young

grasslands dry areas covered with grass where only a few bushes and trees grow

herd a large group of animals that live together

male an elephant that cannot give birth to young

mammals animals that have fur, give birth to live young, and drink milk from their mothers' bodies as babies

mate to come together to have young

matriarch a female who is the head of a family or group

muscles parts of the body that help us move

predators animals that hunt and kill other animals for food

threats things that might cause harm

tusks long, pointed teeth, such as those on an elephant

Index

Read More

Huddleston, Emma. *Elephants (Wild about Animals)*. Minnetonka, MN: Kaleidoscope Publishing, Inc., 2019.

Murray, Julie. *Elephants (Animal Kingdom)*. Minneapolis: ABDO, 2020.

Learn More Online

1. Go to **www.factsurfer.com**
2. Enter "**Elephant**" into the search box.
3. Click on the cover of this book to see a list of websites.

About the Author

Jenna Grodzicki lives on beautiful Cape Cod with her husband and two children. She was a teacher for a long time before she became a writer. She loves to read and go to the beach.